To request permissions, contact the publisher at bczpublishers@gmail.com

Paperback: ISBN 978-1-7367153-6-9

First Paperback Edition: January 2022

Written by: Mina Soliman
Illustrated by: Cynthia Zeilenga

BCZ Publishers
3365 E Miraloma Ave Ste 205, Anaheim, CA 92806

BCZ
PUBLISHERS

how i helped...

Feed the 5,000

"All things are possible for God."
Mark 10:27

I was a very small egg, one of many
Though my destiny was still untold
I felt I had a purpose in this world
A purpose the Lord would soon unfold

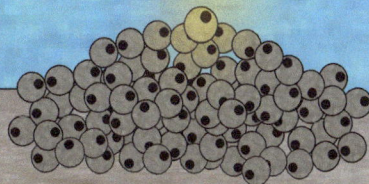

Surrounded by many dangers
A small fish, soon I hatched
While nearby in a manger
A Child was born to which I felt attached

I grew to become a faithful fish
Trusting the Lord with all my might
Knowing that one day I would be called
To help bring many into the light

The Child in the manger also grew
To offer the world salvation
He heard His people's prayers
As they faced much tribulation

Then... On a day that felt much like any other
Something very extraordinary took place
I grew curious as I saw a boat from below
And quickly swam closer as the sun kissed my face

When I reached the surface
I saw a father and his boy
The boy opened his hands, and I quickly swam up
Feeling at that moment such great joy

As Jesus continued to preach throughout the town
His heart was filled with compassion for the starving crowd
The disciples urged Him to send them all away
Instead, He saw a young boy He knew would make Him proud

The young boy humbly offered all he had
A small basket with five loaves and two fish
I had no fear or second thought
For I was about to be granted my heart's wish

Jesus performed an amazing miracle
Multiplying me and the bread to the last crumb
To feed five thousand people
Fully showing the power of His Kingdom come

God revealed my purpose on that incredible day
And as I grew older I finally understood
I willingly gave my life for you to know
The meaning of true sacrifice for the greater good

The End.

PUBLISHERS